THE UN-SPOKEN RULES OF

GOLF ETIQUETTE

A FORMULA TO A FASTER, MORE ENJOYABLE ROUND OF GOLF

AUTHOR
JAMES S. SIMPSON

Copyright 2002 by James Simpson: JP Images of San Diego, Inc.
Library of Congress Card Number: 00-193224

Simpson, James S.
*The Un-Spoken Rules of Golf Etiquette: A formula to a faster,
more enjoyable round of golf.*

ISBN 0-9706744-0-6

Printed in the United States of America

PUBLISHER:
JP IMAGES OF SAN DIEGO
PHOENIX PUBLISHING GROUP

Visit Our Website:
www.mygolfetiquette.com

TEXT CREDITS
Used by permission by Brownlow Corporation,
Ft. Worth, TX 76117

ILLUSTRATIONS
Greg High

PHOTOGRAPHY
Stacy Simpson

Arnold Palmer quote/letter to author: dated June 18, 2001

arn ld palmer

post
office
box
fifty-two
youngstown,
pennsylvania
15696

June 18, 2001

Dear James:

I have read, with interest, your manuscript, *"The Un-Spoken Rules of Golf Etiquette,"* and can assure you that I am in agreement with the views you are expressing in your book.

Proper conduct and courtesies and the honoring of the traditions and rules of the game are vital to its continuing success and popularity.

Thanks for your mailing and good luck with your book.

Sincerely,

Arnold Palmer

AP/dg

James S. Simpson
4414 Salisbury Drive
Carlsbad CA 92008

DAVIS M. LOVE, III
POST OFFICE BOX 30959
SEA ISLAND, GEORGIA 31561

Dear James,

Thanks for the copy of your book, and you can use the the following endorsement as you wish

Before my father let me out on the course alone he taught me all the rules of golf, including Etiquette. This book will be part of my son's golf education for sure. Finally a book that will help all golfers enjoy the game more!

Good luck with the book!

CONTENTS

ANYWHERE ON THE GOLF COURSE

"Mr. Simpson's book should be read by many golfers. Those taking up the game as well as people who have played for years. Its underlying hallmark is consideration for others, which forms the basis for nearly all procedures in golf. Respect other players and the course, and everything should follow."

BEN CRENSHAW

INTRODUCTION

The "Un-Spoken Rules of Golf Etiquette" carry no penalty, no loss of stroke or distance. The rules apply only to etiquette, courtesy and momentum resulting in a faster, more enjoyable round of golf.

How many times have you played golf with friends, strangers, clients, or potential clients and had your round spoiled by the conduct and character of someone in your group? As important as it is to have fun, it is equally important to have good golf etiquette!

How often has slow play affected the enjoyment of your round? Slow play often results from a player's lack of awareness with regard to momentum. Understanding momentum is the key to a faster, more enjoyable round of golf.

"The Un-Spoken Rules of Golf Etiquette" helps to stimulate momentum. From tee to green, let me explain how these rules help speed up play. First, the tee shot. "If your tee shot could be lost or out of bounds, hit a provisional" (Un-Spoken Rule 1-C). This prevents the long trip back to the tee, leaving your playing partners waiting anxiously to hit. Once on the fairway, make sure to "Bring enough clubs when having to walk to a shot" (Un-Spoken Rule 4-C). Walking back to the cart for the right club can really test a group's patience. After reaching the green, mark your ball and begin to "Look at your line while others are putting" (Un-Spoken Rule 9-A). This keeps play moving on the green and helps players maintain their concentration and focus. Remember, always "Be ready to hit when it's your turn" (Un-Spoken Rule 13-C). No matter which fairway, tee or green you're playing from, know when it's your turn and be ready to hit. Without delay, visualize the shot, take a practice swing and hit it. Understanding momentum helps keep your group from falling behind and prevents slow play all the way back to the first tee.

These rules are "Un-Spoken Rules" because most players choose not to mention an infraction as they are violated. Recently, I played with a friend who missed a short putt and smacked his golf ball like a hockey puck, removing a huge divot out of the green. Pointing out proper etiquette is something I wish I could do more comfortably. I believe most golfers would agree. There are uncritical ways to communicate your thoughts while still getting your point across. For example, telling a player "you better wait to hit, I think you can reach the green" is a nice way to say, "I don't want you to hit anyone". Telling someone to be quiet or to hurry up doesn't fit my personality, not to say I haven't come close. The "Un-Spoken Rules of Golf Etiquette" was written to help golfers understand the behaviors which, if followed, result in a faster, more enjoyable round of golf for everyone involved.

Here is a sampling of "The Un-Spoken Rules", which help golfers play quickly and efficiently once reaching the green. First, players should always "Remain at the green until everyone has putted out" (Un-Spoken Rule 7-C). This demonstrates good etiquette. Congratulating a player for sinking a birdie putt is part of the excitement and spirit of the game. If you're the first player to putt out, grab the flagstick and wait for the last person to putt out before you, "Replace the flagstick properly" (Un-Spoken Rule 10-D). Remember, "The last player to putt should not have to replace the flagstick" (Un-Spoken Rule 7-D). The courtesy of replacing the flagstick after the last person putts out is a common example of good etiquette. Then, "Exit the green immediately after completing the hole" (Un-Spoken Rule 12-D). It's very important that players not record scores, replay putts or cause undue delay after the last player putts out. "When approaching the next tee, be aware of players teeing off" (Un-Spoken Rule 2-A). This will insure a courteous and quiet arrival to the next tee. Following this sequence of events should happen automatically and with minimal effort to help keep play moving quickly and efficiently.

Throughout a round of golf, a player's character is tested many different ways. The way in which a player conducts himself or herself on the golf course can translate to behaviors consistent with the outside world.

Someone who plays the first 15 holes like a pro, takes a triple bogey on 16 and then throws a club, may not be the kind of person you thought they were.

Tending the flagstick, replacing a divot or repairing a ball mark are all expected behaviors and signs of good etiquette. When was the last time you were told to be quiet or to replace your divot? Do you remember how you felt? Embarrassed or even insulted? Maybe you were simply unaware of the etiquette. All of us, at some point, have slipped on our etiquette. Nobody's perfect. Certain behaviors players find disruptive may be obvious to some but not to others. "The Un-Spoken Rules of Golf Etiquette" will help you to understand those behaviors players may find distracting or even offensive.

Maintaining proper etiquette throughout a round of golf is difficult. When part of your game has left you, your etiquette should remain intact. The emotional roller coaster of missing putts, hitting balls out of bounds or missing greens is quite a ride. It's during these times a player must rise to the occasion and avoid letting their emotions get the upper hand.

The importance of etiquette has not changed since the game was created. As Arnold Palmer wrote, "Proper conduct and courtesies and the honoring of the traditions and rules of the game are vital to its continuing success and popularity". So true! Honoring the traditions and rules of the game is what makes writing this book so significant. If reading this book gives you a better understanding of the game in regards to etiquette, then my goal has been reached. Honoring the traditions and rules of the game is every player's responsibility. It's a great game and a difficult game, but more important than one's ability is the knowledge of golf etiquette. This knowledge is what helps maintain and preserve the integrity of this great game called, Golf.

"If everyone played the game
concerned more about etiquette,
momentum and the shortest route
to their ball, the time taken
to play 18 holes
would be significantly decreased".

JIM SIMPSON

"Courtesy and integrity are keystones
of the game of golf, and learning the rules
of etiquette is as essential to one's enjoyment
of the game as is learning the fundamentals
of the swing. Jim Simpson has done
an exceptionally thorough job of explaining
The Un-Spoken Rules of Golf Etiquette
in a positive, straightforward style
that will be welcomed by every golfer,
particularly those who are new to the game."

JACK NICKLAUS

The
Un-Spoken Rules
of
Golf
Etiquette

On The Tee

HOLE #1

PAR 4 • 432 YARDS

RULE 1-A
Welcome each player in your group

RULE 1-B
Allow the group ahead to be out
of range before teeing off

RULE 1-C
If your tee shot could be lost
or out of bounds, hit a provisional

Welcome each player in your group

WELCOME EACH PLAYER
IN YOUR GROUP

A round of golf should always begin by welcoming your playing partners with a handshake and a few words of encouragement. The first tee is where you choose your partner, determine who leads off, discuss handicaps and declare the type of ball you're playing, etc. The first tee sets the mood. Make a point to introduce yourself to players whom you haven't met and be ready to hit when it's your turn. Running up to the tee in the nick of time without the introduction sends the wrong message.

Remember,
a good first impression
goes a long way.

*Allow the group ahead to be out
of range before teeing off*

— RULE 1-B —
ALLOW THE GROUP AHEAD TO BE OUT OF RANGE BEFORE TEEING OFF

Allow the group ahead enough time to be out of range before teeing off. If long hitters in the group are able to reach the group ahead, let the shorter hitters tee off first to keep play moving. The time it takes for the players to be out of range is only a matter of a few minutes. Making the mistake of hitting into the group ahead is simply a bad error in judgment. This error in judgment causes tension and can affect how someone plays the next shot.

Remember, yelling "FORE" should be used for a bad shot not a good shot.

*If your tee shot could be lost or
out of bounds, hit a provisional*

IF YOUR TEE SHOT COULD BE LOST OR OUT OF BOUNDS, HIT A PROVISIONAL

Whether you are hitting from the tee or the fairway, hit a provisional if your ball may be lost or close to being out of bounds. Making that long trip back to the tee causes undue delay and can result in your group falling behind. The time it takes to hit a provisional is minimal compared to the delay caused by not hitting one.

Remember, hitting a provisional is your right!

*"To control your nerves,
you must have
a positive thought
in your mind"*

BYRON NELSON

THE UN-SPOKEN RULES OF GOLF ETIQUETTE

ON THE TEE

HOLE #2

PAR 4 • 379 YARDS

RULE 2-A
When approaching the next tee,
be aware of players teeing off

RULE 2-B
Watch everyone tee off

RULE 2-C
Stand still and remain quiet
while players tee off

When approaching the next tee,
be aware of players teeing off

— RULE 2-A —
WHEN APPROACHING THE NEXT TEE, BE AWARE OF PLAYERS TEEING OFF

When approaching the next tee, be careful not to distract players who may be teeing off. Hearing a cart drive up in the middle of your backswing or a player walking toward the tee with clubs rattling can be very distracting. When approaching the next tee, if you see someone in his or her pre-shot routine, wait until the player hits and then proceed. Arriving at the tee while a group is teeing off is okay as long as your approach is courteous. It's all in how you get there that counts.

Remember,
the tee shot is very important.

Watch everyone tee off

— RULE 2-B —
WATCH EVERYONE
TEE OFF

Watch everyone tee off in the event you're asked to help locate a ball. How many times have you heard, "You didn't happen to see where I went, did you?" Looking for golf balls is part of the game. In the rough or around the green, a golf ball can be difficult to locate, and help finding a ball is good etiquette and always appreciated. Watching tee shots reduces the amount of time you spend looking for balls and helps maintain momentum.

Remember,
next time you may
need the help.

Stand still and remain quiet
while players tee off

— RULE 2-C —
STAND STILL AND REMAIN QUIET WHILE PLAYERS TEE OFF

When a player begins the pre-shot routine, avoid making practice swings, pulling clubs or moving in the player's peripheral vision. Talking, whispering or walking during a player's swing can be the difference between a successful tee shot or a shank. Having a quiet tee box allows players the opportunity to concentrate and focus on the shot at hand.

Remember;
Quiet
on the Tee!

*"A bad attitude
is worse than
a bad swing"*

PAYNE STEWART

THE
UN-SPOKEN RULES
OF
GOLF
ETIQUETTE

ON THE TEE

HOLE #3

PAR 3 • 187 YARDS

RULE 3-A
When teeing off on a Par 3, allow
enough time for the green to clear

RULE 3-B
Remain on the tee box
until everyone has teed off

RULE 3-C
Pick up your tee after teeing off

*When teeing off on a Par 3, allow
enough time for the green to clear*

— RULE 3-A —
WHEN TEEING OFF ON A PAR 3, ALLOW ENOUGH TIME FOR THE GREEN TO CLEAR

For the safety of those ahead, always allow enough time for players to be out of range in case you hook, slice or overclub the shot. The time it takes for players to be out of range is only a matter of a few minutes. Hit your tee shot only when it is safe. Shorter hitters may elect to hit when the last person walks off the green. Longer hitters may elect to wait until the group ahead has returned to the carts or have walked completely out of range.

Remember, safety first!

Remain on the tee box
until everyone has teed off

— RULE 3-B —
REMAIN ON THE TEE BOX UNTIL EVERYONE HAS TEED OFF

After hitting your tee shot, remain on the tee box until everyone has hit. Complementing a well struck tee shot demonstrates good etiquette. Walking back to the cart to return your club before everyone has hit can effect how someone plays their shot. Sometimes the sound of returning a club to your bag can be loud and distracting. The proper etiquette is to remain on the tee box, be ready to hit when it's your turn, and watch everyone tee off.

Remember,
the next time you hit
a long drive, a gallery
would be nice.

Pick up your tee after teeing off

— RULE 3-C —
PICK UP YOUR TEE
AFTER TEEING OFF

After hitting your tee shot, pick up your tee. Whether the tee is broken or not, the golf course superintendent would appreciate it if we pick em' up. A player's effort to maintain a clean appearance to the tee box benefits not only the players behind us, but protects the mower blades as well. Most golf courses offer a way to dispose of your tees and trash on every - or almost every - tee box.

Remember,
you may need
that tee later.

*"The reason the
Road Hole is the greatest
par four in the world
is because it's a par five"*

BEN CRENSHAW

THE
UN-SPOKEN RULES
OF
GOLF
ETIQUETTE

IN THE FAIRWAY

HOLE #4

PAR 5 • 512 YARDS

RULE 4-A
When trying to reach a Par 5 in two,
if a career shot is possible, wait

RULE 4-B
Bring enough clubs when having
to walk to a shot

RULE 4-C
If a ball is not easily found, invite
the group following to pass

When trying to reach a Par 5 in two,
if a career shot is possible, wait

— RULE 4-A —
WHEN TRYING TO REACH A PAR 5 IN TWO, IF A CAREER SHOT IS POSSIBLE, WAIT

If you are able to reach a Par 5 in two or drive a Par 4, wait to hit until the green is clear. Flying your ball onto the green where players are putting is dangerous and a sign of poor judgment. Use self control if you're able to reach the green by waiting to hit. Jeopardizing the safety of the group ahead is not worth a moment of glory. Seeing a ball roll through your legs while preparing to putt or hearing "FORE" from the fairway can ruin your concentration and focus.

Remember, reaching Par 5's in two or driving Par 4's is awesome, so keep it that way!

Bring enough clubs when
having to walk to a shot

— RULE 4-B —
BRING ENOUGH CLUBS
WHEN HAVING TO WALK
TO A SHOT

I f walking from the cart to your shot is a considerable distance, bring enough clubs. If you feel your next shot requires a 5-iron, bring a 4 and a 6-iron just in case. The situation you avoid is having to return to the cart for the right club leaving your playing partners in a state of limbo. This affects the group's momentum and increases the risk of falling behind.

Remember,
one under and one
over the number.

If a ball is not easily found,
invite the group following to pass

— RULE 4-C —
IF A BALL IS NOT EASILY FOUND, INVITE THE GROUP FOLLOWING TO PASS

As a courtesy to those playing with you and behind you, look in bounds first and out of bounds last. If it becomes necessary, declare your ball lost and quickly proceed to your provisional. You're allowed five minutes to find your ball. If you determine your ball cannot easily be found, do not take the full five minutes before allowing the group following to pass. If you find your ball out of bounds and haven't hit a provisional, the rules of golf dictate you must return to the spot where you last played your shot. Players who wish to post a legitimate score for handicap purposes must return. This is why hitting a provisional is so important.

Remember,
time is crucial to everyone's
enjoyment of the game.

47

"Never needle, harass or poke fun at a playing partner who's on the edge of despair"

DOUG SANDERS

THE
UN-SPOKEN RULES
OF
GOLF
ETIQUETTE

IN THE FAIRWAY

HOLE #5

PAR 4 • 398 YARDS

RULE 5-A
If your score becomes
a non-issue, pick it up

RULE 5-B
Avoid "ball to ball" service
when riding a cart

RULE 5-C
Be responsible for damage
caused by an errant shot

If your score becomes a
non-issue, pick it up

IF YOUR SCORE BECOMES A NON-ISSUE, PICK IT UP

While playing a hole, if your score becomes excessively high and you're "out of the hole", pick it up. A player who reads a putt from both sides when putting for a 10 is showing very poor etiquette. In determining a player's "index" the USGA implements the Equitable Stroke Control formula which determines the maximum score a player is allowed on any particular hole consistent with a player's current index. This chart can be found at your local golf course or country club where scores are posted. If you are unable to locate this chart for any reason, contact the United States Golf Association. These limits help keep the game moving and prevent groups from falling behind.

Remember, enough is enough.

Avoid "ball to ball" service
when riding a cart

— RULE 5-B —
AVOID "BALL TO BALL" SERVICE WHEN RIDING A CART

Whether you're the driver or the passenger, don't wait to be driven to each shot. If your ball is within walking distance, estimate the yardage, bring enough clubs and walk to your shot. This helps keep your group moving forward. Sitting in the cart waiting to be driven to a ball within walking distance causes undue delay and affects the momentum of the group.

*Remember,
anticipate your next shot,
walk when you can
and be ready to hit.*

Be responsible for damage
caused by an errant shot

— RULE 5-C —
BE RESPONSIBLE FOR DAMAGE CAUSED BY AN ERRANT SHOT

If, during the round, your ball ends up through a window or the golf cart ends up in a lake, take responsibility. Nowadays, homes are built in such close proximity to fairways and greens that the chances of causing damage have been greatly increased. If you're guilty, at the conclusion of your round, give the pro shop your name, phone number and how you can be contacted. This allows the golf course to forward your information to the appropriate parties.

Remember,
it's the right thing to do.

*"You must work
very hard to become
a natural golfer"*

GARY PLAYER

THE
UN-SPOKEN RULES
OF
GOLF
ETIQUETTE

IN THE FAIRWAY

HOLE #6

PAR 4 • 401 YARDS

RULE 6-A
Avoid walking out in front
of a player while hitting

RULE 6-B
Honor the 90 degree rule
when driving a cart

*Avoid walking out in front
of a player while hitting*

— RULE 6-A —
AVOID WALKING OUT IN FRONT OF A PLAYER WHILE HITTING

Walking out in front of a player making an approach shot demonstrates poor etiquette. It's okay to be out in front of a player hitting as long as you're off to the side and remain still. Knowing where you are in relation to other players on the hole will prevent this from happening. When a player begins a pre-shot routine or addresses the ball, wait for the hit, then proceed. Show an interest in other players by watching their shots. Having to listen to player's clubs rattle as they walk down the fairway badly affects the concentration required to make a good swing.

Remember,
it's easier to duck
if you see it coming.

Honor the 90 degree rule
when driving a cart

— RULE 6-B —
HONOR THE 90 DEGREE RULE
WHEN DRIVING A CART

The purpose of the 90 degree rule is to protect the fairways from being run over by carts. The weight of these vehicles punishes the turf and can make life miserable for the golf course superintendent. When signs are posted to honor the 90 degree rule, it means to drive on the cart paths parallel to the fairway until you reach the point where a 90 degree turn will take you to your ball. Also, keep carts a considerable distance (at least 30 feet) from tee boxes and greens. This will help keep the golf course in the kind of shape you like to see it in.

Remember,
keep it
in the rough.

"There are putters and putters.
If a man putts poorly it isn't so much
the fault of the club as of the putter.
A naturally good putter will
putt fairly well with any old weapon.
At the same time, I am of the
opinion that the best results
can be secured by a putting cleek
with a short shaft"

WALTER J. TRAVIS
U.S. Amateur Champion 1900, 1901, 1903
British Amateur Champion 1904

THE
UN-SPOKEN RULES
OF
GOLF
ETIQUETTE

ON OR AROUND
THE GREEN

HOLE #7

PAR 3 • 167 YARDS

RULE 7-A
Avoid talking while a player is putting

RULE 7-B
After hitting from a bunker,
rake the bunker

RULE 7-C
Remain at the green
until everyone has putted out

RULE 7-D
The last person to putt should not
have to replace the flagstick

*Avoid talking while
a player is putting*

— RULE 7-A —
AVOID TALKING WHILE
A PLAYER IS PUTTING

When a player begins the pre-shot routine, all conversations should cease. Reducing your voice to a whisper is not being quiet. The concentration required to make a good putting stroke can easily be interrupted by players talking or even whispering. If someone in your group is a talker, and it becomes necessary, a simple hand gesture at the appropriate time will get the message across.

Remember, whispering is not being quiet.

After hitting from a bunker,
rake the bunker

— RULE 7-B —
AFTER HITTING FROM A
BUNKER, RAKE THE BUNKER

Arriving to a bunker shot only to see your ball sitting in someone's footprint is aggravating to say the least. Show good etiquette by always raking the bunker after a bunker shot. To help speed up play and reduce the time necessary to rake, always enter the bunker at a point closest to your ball as long as you don't enter from the top of the lip. Also, locate the rake before entering the bunker and bring it with you. If possible, while raking your own footprints, rake other footprints as long as you don't hold up play in doing so. Also, the noise created when raking a bunker can be a distraction to another player preparing to hit their next shot. Be aware!

Remember,
hitting from a bunker
is hard enough!

Remain at the green until
everyone has putted out

— RULE 7-C —
REMAIN AT THE GREEN
UNTIL EVERYONE HAS
PUTTED OUT

A common courtesy to your playing partners is to remain at the green until the last player putts out. Be there to congratulate a great putt. Show an interest in other players' games. This is what the game of golf is all about. Watching players leave the green when standing over a birdie putt is not in the spirit of the game.

Remember,
a birdie feels a lot
better with a gallery.

The last player to putt should not
have to replace the flagstick

— RULE 7-D —
THE LAST PLAYER TO PUTT
SHOULD NOT HAVE TO
REPLACE THE FLAGSTICK

Make sure the last person putting isn't left to grab the flagstick. Walking to the next tee while a member of your group is still putting shows poor etiquette. Demonstrate courtesy to the members of your group by picking up clubs and towels to help your group exit the green quickly. The first player to putt out should retrieve the flagstick and be ready to replace it when the last player putts out. Showing good etiquette and consideration around the green helps speed up play.

Remember,
don't be afraid
to pick up the flagstick!

*"Feel brave
if you lose and meek
if you win"*

HARVEY PENICK

THE
UN-SPOKEN RULES
OF
GOLF
ETIQUETTE

ON OR AROUND
THE GREEN

HOLE #8

PAR 5 • 522 YARDS

RULE 8-A
Be courteous when
removing your glove

RULE 8-B
Mark your ball on the green

RULE 8-C
Repair your ball mark and others

Be courteous when
removing your glove

— RULE 8-A —
BE COURTEOUS WHEN REMOVING YOUR GLOVE

I f you are a player who removes your glove prior to putting, make sure you do so before it becomes your turn to putt. Most importantly, the timing of when to remove your glove is crucial. Hearing the sound of velcro being ripped apart in the middle of the takeaway can startle even the best putters. There have been many missed putts and errant shots blamed over the removal of a golf glove. Show consideration to your fellow golfer by removing your glove at the appropriate time.

Remember,
timing is everything.

Mark your ball on the green

— RULE 8-B —
MARK YOUR BALL
ON THE GREEN

After reaching the green, always mark your ball. Marking your ball shows consideration to the player who is putting and also gives you a chance to clean your ball. Standing over a putt and seeing a ball resting close to the hole is distracting.

Remember,
a clear putting surface
is soothing to the eye.

Repair your ball mark and others

— RULE 8-C —
REPAIR YOUR BALL
MARK AND OTHERS

After arriving on the green, repair your ball mark. Fixing ball marks is a privilege. Some players can't wait until they make one! Without holding up play, repair other ball marks if time allows. The time required to fix a ball mark is insignificant to the time it takes a green to heal from its wounds. In the long run, the effects of not fixing ball marks results in slow play. Why? Because most players will repair ball marks in their line of putt. Have you ever noticed when playing on perfect greens how most of your time is spent looking at the line rather than fixing ball marks?

Remember, that ball mark
might be in your line
next time around!

"Correct one fault at a time. Concentrate on the one fault you want to overcome"

SAM SNEAD

THE
UN-SPOKEN RULES
OF
GOLF
ETIQUETTE

ON OR AROUND
THE GREEN

HOLE #9

PAR 4 • 388 YARDS

RULE 9-A
Look at your line
while others are putting

RULE 9-B
Watch your shadow

RULE 9-C
Avoid stepping on
a player's line of putt

81

Look at your line
while others are putting

— RULE 9-A —
LOOK AT YOUR LINE WHILE OTHERS ARE PUTTING

While waiting to putt, look at your line while others are putting. Moving from one side of your line to the other can be done without disturbing other players. Not only does this help speed up play around the green but helps maintain the momentum necessary to stay focused. What you want to avoid, is being the last to putt and looking at the line from both sides.

Remember,
being ready to putt when it
becomes your turn helps
everyone concentrate.

Watch your shadow

— RULE 9-B —
WATCH YOUR SHADOW

Make sure your shadow doesn't cross a player's line of putt. When a player's shadow is crossing another player's line, it's usually on accident. Shadows at the end of a day can get long and reach a considerable distance across the green. Not only should players watch their shadows around the green but also on the tee box and fairway as well.

Remember,
follow your shadow
and you'll be fine.

*Avoid stepping on
a player's line of putt*

— RULE 9-C —
AVOID STEPPING ON A PLAYER'S LINE OF PUTT

Not often during a round of golf does a player step on your line. If a player happens to step on your line, he or she is usually unaware of the etiquette or is simply not paying attention. Once on the green, get a feel for where everyone is in relation to your ball. This will not only help you avoid this breech of etiquette but will also give you an idea of who's next to play.

Remember,
be aware of other
player's lines.

Making The Turn

MAKING THE TURN

When making the turn, be sure not to fall out of position. Ordering food, going to the restroom, adding up scores, etc., should be done quickly and without delay. If your group elects to order food resulting in your group falling behind, invite the group following to pass. This keeps play moving and displays good etiquette. Coming off the 9th green and seeing a backup on the 10th tee is a golfers' nightmare. Be courteous to players following your group by making the turn quickly. If a snack bar phone is available on the 9th tee box, place your orders there.

Remember, nothing well done.

"Every golfer can expect to have four bad shots a round. When you do, just put them out of your mind"

WALTER HAGEN

THE
UN-SPOKEN RULES
OF
GOLF
ETIQUETTE

ON OR AROUND
THE GREEN

HOLE #10

PAR 5 • 532 YARDS

RULE 10-A
After reaching the green,
pay attention to those who haven't

RULE 10-B
Closest to the flagstick either
tends or pulls the flagstick

RULE 10-C
Don't remark your ball
until it is your turn to putt

RULE 10-D
Replace the flagstick properly

91

After reaching the green,
pay attention to those who haven't

— RULE 10-A —
AFTER REACHING THE GREEN, PAY ATTENTION TO THOSE WHO HAVEN'T

When arriving at the green, check to see that all in your group have played their shots to the green before walking onto the putting surface. Players who have yet to reach the green may be hitting from positions difficult to see. You never know if someone may be hitting from the trees or a deep bunker. If you notice a player addressing the ball, remain still and wait for the player to hit, then proceed to mark your ball.

*Remember,
make sure the
coast is clear.*

Closest to the flagstick either
tends or pulls the flagstick

— RULE 10-B —
CLOSEST TO THE FLAGSTICK EITHER TENDS OR PULLS THE FLAGSTICK

When arriving to the green, the player closest to the flagstick is responsible for pulling or tending the flag. The proper way to tend the flagstick is to stand on the side where your shadow is cast. Don't allow your shadow to cross the line of the player putting. In some cases, players may be just off the green and ask the flagstick to be pulled. After pulling the flagstick, lay it down gently and without damaging the putting surface. A flagstick can damage the green quite easily when tossed or thrown. Place the flagstick away from a player's line of putt and the "through line" which is the putting surface beyond the hole on a player's line. Be courteous as to when and how you handle a flagstick.

Remember, closest to the flagstick tends the flagstick.

*Don't remark your ball until
it is your turn to putt*

— RULE 10-C —
DON'T REMARK YOUR BALL UNTIL IT IS YOUR TURN TO PUTT

After marking your ball on the green, don't remark your ball until it becomes your turn to putt. The purpose of marking your ball on the green is to give your playing partners a clear putting surface. Seeing a player replace their ball on the green before his or her turn to putt signals an intent to putt. This temporary state of confusion is a distraction to the player ready to putt. Having to make comments such as, "I think I'm out", or "If you're ready, go ahead" generally will bring the situation back to order. Granted, this rule does not apply to a player who is replacing the ball directly in back of a player who is putting. Obviously, remarking your ball behind someone is not a distraction; in fact, this speeds up play on the green and is recommended. This rule concerns the golfer who replaces the ball in close proximity to the hole before it becomes his or her turn to putt.

Remember, one ball in sight at a time.

Replace the flagstick properly

— RULE 10-D —
REPLACE THE FLAGSTICK PROPERLY

Before leaving the green, be sure to replace the flagstick firmly into the bottom of the cup. Also, when lifting or replacing the flagstick, be careful not to damage the edge of the cup. The edge of the cup can be easily damaged when struck by the base of a flagstick. Players who aggressively replace the flagstick risk damaging the cup's edge. Making sure players who still need to putt have a round hole is every player's responsibility.

Remember,
keep it down
the center.

*"Never break your putter
and your driver
in the same round
or you're dead"*

TOMMY BOLT

THE
UN-SPOKEN RULES
OF
GOLF
ETIQUETTE

ON OR AROUND
THE GREEN

HOLE #11

PAR 3 • 177 YARDS

RULE 11-A
Don't remove your ball from
the hole with your putter head

RULE 11-B
Don't strike the putting
surface after missing a putt

RULE 11-C
Don't stand directly behind or
down the line of a player putting

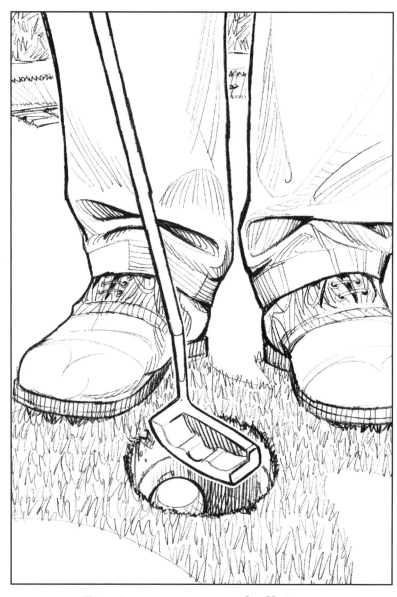

*Don't remove your ball from
the hole with your putter head*

— RULE 11-A —
DON'T REMOVE YOUR BALL
FROM THE HOLE WITH
YOUR PUTTER HEAD

Removing your ball with your putter head can easily damage the edge of the cup. There are gadgets designed specifically for removing your ball if you need assistance. The putter head was not designed for the purpose of removing balls from the hole.

*Remember,
every good putt deserves
a chance to fall.*

*Don't strike the putting surface
after missing a putt*

— RULE 11-B —
DON'T STRIKE
THE PUTTING SURFACE
AFTER MISSING A PUTT

How many times have you seen a player hammer the putting surface after missing a putt? Whether it's a long or short putt, the putting surface seems to take the abuse. Putting greens are the most expensive area on the golf course, as well as the most difficult to maintain. It can take weeks, months or even longer for a green to repair itself from ball marks and damage caused by outside forces. The golf course superintendent is ultimately affected. Golf course superintendents are judged by how well a golf course is maintained and the playability of its fairways and greens. This person's job is literally on the line each time a golf course has problems. Showing respect to the golf course by restraining oneself during moments of lip outs is every player's responsibility. Repairing your ball marks and replacing your divots demonstrate consideration not only for your fellow players but for the personnel who strive each day to make sure your putts roll true.

Remember, it's not the greens fault.

Don't stand directly behind or
down the line of a player putting

— RULE 11-C —
DON'T STAND DIRECTLY
BEHIND OR DOWN THE LINE
OF A PLAYER PUTTING

When a player begins the pre-shot routine, make sure you're not standing directly behind or down the intended line of putt. If you find yourself in this position, sometimes you will be asked to move out of the player's peripheral vision. Seeing a player standing directly down your line can sometimes affect your ability to concentrate. It's a simple mistake and is easily rectified. Some players are not bothered by this. They simply will go ahead and make their stroke. Proper etiquette requires that you stand to the side and away from the intended line of putt.

Remember,
don't go to school on
another player's putt.

"I consider putting,
next to the mashie approach,
the most important stroke in golf.
I always carry two
different kinds of putters
and I have several different stances,
and if I am off with one putter
I try the other and
keep altering my stance
until I feel perfectly comfortable;
for without this feeling you cannot have
confidence, and without confidence
good and accurate putting
is an impossibility"

HARRY VARDON

THE
UN-SPOKEN RULES
OF
GOLF
ETIQUETTE

ON OR AROUND
THE GREEN

HOLE #12

PAR 4 • 426 YARDS

RULE 12-A
Remain still while a player is putting

RULE 12-B
Remove your ball from the hole
after finishing out

RULE 12-C
Leave the green immediately
after completing the hole

Remain still while a player is putting

— RULE 12-A —
REMAIN STILL WHILE A
PLAYER IS PUTTING

When a player begins the pre-shot routine and eventual putting stroke, refrain from walking, stretching, juggling your golf ball or any other motion that can be detected in a player's peripheral vision. All players have a different range of peripheral vision. What one player may see, another player may not. Make sure when a player addresses their ball, all movement and conversations cease.

Remember,
next time you may
be the one putting.

Remove your ball from the hole
after finishing out

— RULE 12-B —
REMOVE YOUR BALL
FROM THE HOLE
AFTER FINISHING OUT

After putting your ball in the hole, proceed to the cup and retrieve your ball. Celebrating after sinking a putt while leaving the ball in the hole is poor etiquette. Some players may not be distracted by this, but other players are.

*Remember,
one's company
two's a crowd.*

*Leave the green immediately
after completing the hole*

LEAVE THE GREEN IMMEDIATELY AFTER COMPLETING THE HOLE

After the last player putts out, immediately replace the flagstick and exit the green. If you are walking, leave your bag on the path you will use in exiting the green. Walking to the opposite side of the green to retrieve your bag delays your exit and is poor planning. Be sure to exit the green completely and be out of range prior to writing down scores. Recording scores should be done on or around the next tee and without slowing down play. This allows those in the group following to make their approach shots without undue delay.

Remember,
replace the flagstick
and talk as you walk.

*"It is nothing new or
original to say that golf
is played one stroke at a time.
But it took me years
to realize it"*

BOBBY JONES

THE UN-SPOKEN RULES OF GOLF ETIQUETTE

ANYWHERE ON THE GOLF COURSE

HOLE #13

PAR 4 • 394 YARDS

RULE 13-A
Keep practice swings
to a minimum

RULE 13-B
Avoid hitting out of turn

RULE 13-C
Be ready to hit when it's your turn

Keep practice swings to a minimum

— RULE 13-A —
KEEP PRACTICE SWINGS
TO A MINIMUM

When preparing to hit from the tee, fairway or when on the green, practice swings are taken to develop tempo and a sense of rhythm. For most golfers, practice swings are part of the game. During your pre-shot routine, avoid taking more than 1 or 2 practice swings. This is not a hard fast rule but it's all that is necessary to gain what practice swings have to offer. Players who take 4 or 5 practice swings before each shot need to understand they are adversely affecting the group's momentum. Excessive practice swings contribute to slow play and over time can cause a group to fall out of position.

Remember,
take a practice swing,
visualize the shot and hit it.

Avoid hitting out of turn

— RULE 13-B —
AVOID HITTING OUT OF TURN

The player furthest away from the green hits first. A player who hits out of turn is showing very poor etiquette and is a distraction to others who may be preparing to hit. Be aware of your position in relation to other players and make sure it's your turn to hit. If your group is playing "Ready Golf", make sure before you hit no other player is hitting at the same time.

**Remember,
the player furthest
away is next to play.**

Be ready to hit when it's your turn

— RULE 13-C —
BE READY TO HIT WHEN
IT'S YOUR TURN

B eing ready to hit when it's your turn is one of the most important courtesies you can afford your playing partners. Maintaining momentum and avoiding slow play is every player's responsibility. Talking on a cellular phone, or sitting in the cart when it comes your turn, slows down the group as well as the entire golf course. Be aware of your position on each hole. Whatever your pre-shot routine includes, attempt to walk off yardage, select a club and take practice swings before it becomes your turn to play.

Remember,
being ready to play
helps cure slow play.

"Keep your sense of humor.
There's enough stress
in the rest of your life
to let bad shots ruin a game
you're supposed to enjoy"

AMY ALCOTT

THE
UN-SPOKEN RULES
OF
GOLF
ETIQUETTE

ANYWHERE ON THE
GOLF COURSE

HOLE #14

PAR 5 • 546 YARDS

RULE 14-A
Pay attention when releasing
the brake pedal

RULE 14-B
Be courteous when returning
or pulling clubs

RULE 14-C
Remain quiet while a player is hitting

Pay attention when releasing
the brake pedal

— RULE 14-A —
PAY ATTENTION WHEN RELEASING THE BRAKE PEDAL

How many times has a player released the brake pedal at the top of your swing? The loud noise generated by releasing the brake pedal is a sound that can be heard from quite a distance. Hearing this noise in the middle of your swing can be a good excuse for a bad shot. Always look to see if players are hitting before releasing the brake. Whether your departing or arriving to a shot, golf carts create noises that players find distracting.

Remember,
a cart is only
as quiet as the
person driving it.

*Be courteous when returning
or pulling clubs*

— RULE 14-B —
BE COURTEOUS
WHEN RETURNING OR
PULLING CLUBS

Prior to pulling or replacing a club to your bag, make sure to time it while other players within close proximity are not addressing or hitting a shot. Over the course of 18 holes, pulling and returning clubs to your bag is commonplace activity. The sound and clubs banging together when being returned to the bag can affect how someone hits their shot.

Remember,
metal on metal
is not a good sound.

Remain quiet while a player is hitting

— RULE 14-C —
REMAIN QUIET WHILE
A PLAYER IS HITTING

Talking or whispering while a player is hitting is poor etiquette. Players sometimes strike up a conversation just as other players are about to hit. Be considerate of the timing when to tell a joke or start a conversation. There will be numerous opportunities during a round of golf, when it is appropriate to converse without affecting the player hitting, the speed of play or the momentum of the group. Give the player hitting the courtesy of peace and quiet from the start of the pre-shot routine to the moment of impact. Allowing the player to think only about the shot at hand demonstrates good etiquette.

*Remember,
jokes are a lot more
humorous when there's
time for the punch line.*

*"Golf is a game of
finding what works, losing it,
and finding it again"*

KEN VENTURI

THE UN-SPOKEN RULES OF GOLF ETIQUETTE

ANYWHERE ON THE GOLF COURSE

HOLE #15

PAR 4 • 403 YARDS

RULE 15-A
Be courteous about the use
of a cellular phone

RULE 15-B
If your group falls behind,
play "Ready Golf"

RULE 15-C
Avoid holding up play
by giving golf instruction

133

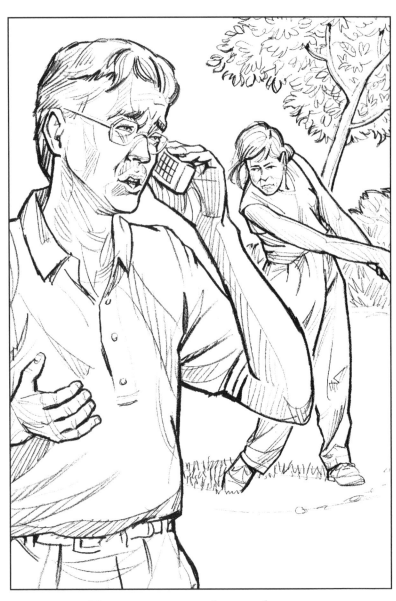

*Be courteous about the use
of a cellular phone*

— RULE 15-A —
BE COURTEOUS ABOUT THE USE OF A CELLULAR PHONE

A major disruption on the golf course is the cellular phone. Listening to someone dispatch their entire work force during a round of golf is highly disruptive and slows down the group as well as the entire golf course. Watching a player run off the green to catch a phone call is irritating. Playing golf with others who constantly have a phone in their ear can be a real challenge. Prior to teeing off, turn your phone off. If you must remain connected to the outside world, place the phone where it causes the least amount of distraction. Cellular phones offer some of us the freedom to be on the golf course but they do not take the place of etiquette and consideration to your fellow golfers. Cellular phones may one day be banned from all golf courses because of the negative impact they have on the speed and enjoyment of play.

Remember, if it's that important you shouldn't be out there.

If your group falls behind,
play "Ready Golf"

— RULE 15-B —
IF YOUR GROUP FALLS
BEHIND, PLAY "READY GOLF"

If at any time during the round your group falls behind or is out of position, play "Ready Golf". "Ready Golf" allows each player the opportunity to hit when ready regardless of who is furthest away or who has the honors. If you can't see the group ahead of you, it's a good time to start playing "Ready Golf". Make sure before you swing that you're not swinging in unison with another player. Playing "Ready Golf" enables your group to get back into position and resume the honor system. If your group is unable to get back into position, allow the group following to pass. This attention to etiquette is what makes a round of golf more enjoyable for everyone.

Remember,
not seeing the group ahead
means you're out of position.

Avoid holding up play
by giving golf instruction

— RULE 15-C —
AVOID HOLDING UP PLAY BY
GIVING GOLF INSTRUCTION

If a playing partner asks for advice, offer it, as long as it doesn't hold up play. Having to wait while someone points out swing flaws slows down play and effects the momentum of the group. There are players who feel the need unsolicited to demonstrate the swing or offer advice. Offer advice only when asked. Some players don't like advice and would prefer you save it for the range.

*Remember,
offer advice only
when asked.*

"Proper conduct and courtesies and the honoring of the traditions and rules of the game are vital to its continuing success and popularity"

ARNOLD PALMER

THE UN-SPOKEN RULES OF GOLF ETIQUETTE

ANYWHERE ON THE GOLF COURSE

HOLE #16

PAR 3 • 196 YARDS

RULE 16-A
Always yell "FORE"

RULE 16-B
Never throw clubs

RULE 16-C
Resist using abusive language

RULE 16-C
Use good judgment
when operating a cart

Always yell "FORE"

— RULE 16-A —
ALWAYS YELL
"FORE"

Anywhere on the golf course, if you see a ball heading toward other players, yell "FORE". Yelling "FORE" gives players the opportunity to duck, hide or simply be aware that a golf ball is heading their way. By not yelling "FORE" you place other players in harms way and increase the chance of someone being injured.

Remember,
yell "FORE" even if you
didn't hit the shot

Never throw clubs!

— RULE 16-B —
NEVER
THROW CLUBS

Never throw clubs! Throwing clubs creates an uncomfortable atmosphere for all involved. Not only does it show a lack of character but a club can cause serious injury if someone accidentally gets hit. Many times throughout your golfing career you'll get frustrated on the golf course. Players who throw clubs must understand the consequences. Not getting invited back may be one of them. The respect you once had in the eyes of others has now, all of a sudden, disappeared. Throwing clubs is inconsiderate, demonstrates poor sportsmanship and, most serious of all, is dangerous.

Remember, the golfing community looks down on this type of behavior and so do your fellow players.

Resist using abusive language

— RULE 16-C —
RESIST USING
ABUSIVE LANGUAGE

Profanity on the golf course is never called for. The misery of lip outs and errant shots can sometimes bring out the worst in us. The biggest concern about profane and abusive language is not knowing who may find it offensive. Being considerate to those around you is what makes golf such a great sport. Golf is a gentlemen's game and is played with a code of conduct based on a long tradition of courtesy. Profanity has no place on the golf course. If you feel you must utter profanity during a round, mutter under your breath so nobody else can hear you.

Remember,
you never know who
may be listening.

Use good judgment
when operating a cart

— RULE 16-D —
USE GOOD JUDGMENT
WHEN OPERATING A CART

On golf courses throughout the world, many serious accidents involving the use of golf carts have occurred. Performing 360's, slamming on the brakes and accelerating to unsafe speeds are but a few examples of reckless behavior and improper operation. Letting everyone know you've arrived to your shot by slamming on the brakes is inconsiderate, disruptive and is detrimental to the golf course. Be respectful to those around you by operating the cart with the least amount of noise and distraction. Golf carts cause serious injury to persons or property if not operated properly.

Remember,
leave the golf course
in one piece.

"Successful competitors
want to win.
Head cases want to win
at all costs."

NANCY LOPEZ

The
Un-Spoken Rules
of
Golf
Etiquette

Anywhere On The
Golf Course

HOLE #17

PAR 4 • 411 YARDS

RULE 17-A
Avoid taking too long over each shot

RULE 17-B
Don't stand directly behind
a player making a stroke

RULE 17-C
If your ball ends up
on an adjacent fairway,
check for golfers playing the hole.

Avoid taking too long
over each shot

— RULE 17-A —
AVOID TAKING TOO LONG
OVER EACH SHOT

P rior to hitting a golf shot, three things should occur: Establishing yardage, club selection, and practice swings. Slow play usually occurs during one of the above. Once you have selected your club and begun your pre-shot routine, take a practice swing, focus on your target and hit it. Taking an excessive amount of time preparing to hit each shot is inconsiderate, disruptive and effects the momentum of the group.

Remember,
momentum is
everything.

*Don't stand directly behind
a player making a stroke*

— RULE 17-B —
DON'T STAND DIRECTLY BEHIND A PLAYER MAKING A STROKE

When a player begins a pre-shot routine, move out from behind the ball and away from the player's peripheral vision. The proper place to stand while a player makes a stroke is off to the side and behind the right angle of the intended line of flight. The rule is to stay out of the peripheral vision of a player making a stroke.

Remember,
watch players from
the side and not behind.

If your ball ends up on an adjacent
fairway, check for golfers playing the hole

— RULE 17-C —
IF YOUR BALL ENDS UP ON AN ADJACENT FAIRWAY, CHECK FOR GOLFERS PLAYING THE HOLE

Many golf courses are designed with fairways adjacent to one another. If you find your tee shot or any subsequent shot on the opposite fairway, pay attention to who may be teeing off or hitting from that fairway before approaching your ball. Forcing a player to back off a shot is simply the result of not paying attention. If you see a group preparing to hit from another hole, wait for the right time to approach your ball. Make members of your group aware of your intention to wait so they can hit their shots without undue delay. When the coast is clear, proceed to your ball and hit it. The most important thing to remember is to be aware of where you are at all times on the golf course so your actions don't cause other players to lose their concentration.

Remember, you're not the only one out there.

"My Philosophy?
Practice, practice
practice—and win"

BABE DIDRIKSON ZAHARIAS

THE
UN-SPOKEN RULES
OF
GOLF
ETIQUETTE

ANYWHERE ON THE
GOLF COURSE

HOLE #18

PAR 4 • 418 YARDS

RULE 18-A
Avoid taking divots
during practice swings

RULE 18-B
Replace your divots

RULE 18-C
Shake hands with your group
after completing the round

Avoid taking divots
during practice swings

— RULE 18-A —
AVOID TAKING DIVOTS
DURING PRACTICE SWINGS

When taking practice swings, try not to take divots. Regardless of where you are, always attempt to sweep or skim the grass when taking practice swings. Par 3's take the majority of abuse when it comes to damage caused by practice swings since most tee shots are made with irons. If you do happen to take a divot or two, always replace them. Also, when riding in a cart, take the sand and seed mixture provided on each cart to the tee in order to save time repairing the divots.

Remember,
the golf course
superintendent's job
is tough enough.

Replace your divots

— RULE 18-B —
REPLACE
YOUR DIVOTS

Always replace your divots. Most golf carts offer a mixture of sand and seed which is used to repair the scar left by a divot. First, attempt to replace the original divot and then sprinkle some sand and seed mixture around the edges to help grow parts of the divot that are missing. If the divot is not replaceable, meaning that the divot is badly damaged and the possibility of it maturing is slim, then fill in the scar completely with sand and seed. A properly replaced divot will often grow back with no real damage to the fairway. This helps to maintain the appearance of the course and taking care of the golf course is every player's responsibility!

Remember, it might be your own divot you're in next time around.

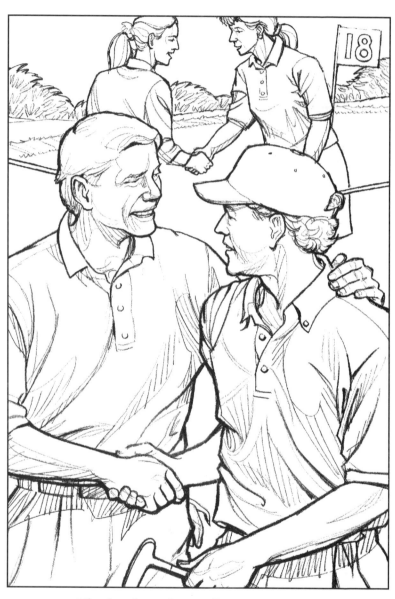

Shake hands with your group
after completing the round

SHAKE HANDS WITH YOUR GROUP AFTER COMPLETING THE ROUND

At the completion of every round, exit the green first, then shake hands with your playing partners. Regardless of how the day went, a golf round should always end with a handshake. This is one of the great things about golf: it begins with a handshake and ends with a handshake. Leaving the golf course any other way sends the wrong message.

*Remember,
a lasting impression
goes a long way.*

"The Un-Spoken Rules
of Golf Etiquette carry no penalty,
no loss of stroke or distance.
The rules apply only to etiquette,
courtesy and momentum,
resulting in a faster,
more enjoyable round of golf"

JAMES SIMPSON

THANKS

I dedicate this book to my best friend and wife, Stacy, who has supported me through my love for the game and has given us our two beautiful daughters, Stevie and Riley.

Thanks to some of the greatest and best known players in the world who took the time to read and offer their names in support of "The Un-Spoken Rules of Golf Etiquette".

Thanks to Jack Nicklaus for an endorsement I'll never forget.

Thanks to Arnold Palmer whose words of encouragement from the beginning, on the subject of etiquette, assured me I was on the right path.

Thanks to David Fay, Executive Director of the United States Golf Association for being a true gentleman and supporting my efforts.

Thanks to Tim Finchem, Commissioner of the PGA TOUR, who wrote a wonderful endorsement.

Thanks to my good friend, and golfing partner, Paul Hornsveld, who loves the game as much as I do.

Thanks to all my friends and customers who I've played with over the years.

Thanks to Rob Roessler for all his input, time and consideration.

Thanks-
James Simpson

GLOSSARY

ADDRESS
The position taken by a player in preparing to make a stroke.

ALTERNATE SHOT
A format in which partners take turns from tee to green until the ball is holed out.

AMATEUR
An amateur golfer is one who plays for fun and relaxation and not for money.

APRON
Associated with the first cut of rough around the putting surface.

BAG DROP
A designated area where you leave your golf bag when arriving at the course.

BALL MARK
The scar or indentation made when a golf ball lands on the putting surface.

BETTER BALL OF PARTNERS
The best score taken between partners on the same hole.

BIRDIE
Score for a hole played in one stroke under par.

BLIND SHOT
Making a stroke to a green or fairway and not being able to see the result due to elevation or a dog leg.

BOGEY
Score for a hole played in one stroke over par.

BREAK
The way in which a putt will move due to the contour of the green.

BUNKER
A bunker is a located anywhere on the golf course, usually in the fairway or around the green where sand has been replaced for turf. A bunker is a "hazard".

CADDIE
A caddie is someone who carries clubs, offers advice and assists a player during a round.

CART
A vehicle used to transport players and equipment during a round of golf.

CART BARN
A secure place where carts are kept.

CASUAL WATER
A temporary accumulation of water located on the golf course that is visible before and after a player takes their stance and is not in a water hazard.

CHAMPIONSHIP TEES
A tee location normally furthest back generally played by low handicap golfers.

CUT SHOT

A ball travelling from left to right for a right-handed golfer and right to left for a left-handed golfer.

DIVOT

Displaced turf that results from striking a golf ball.

DOG LEG

A golf hole that makes a turn to the left or right from the tee.

DOUBLE BOGEY

Score for a hole played in two strokes over par.

DOUBLE EAGLE

Score for a hole played in three strokes under par.

DRAW

A ball flight that travels from right to left for a right-handed golfer or left to right for a left-handed golfer.

DRIVING RANGE

A place where golfers practice their swing or stroke.

FAIRWAY

The portion of terrain between the tee and green which is well kept to provide a favorable lie for the ball.

FIRST OFF

The first group off to start the day.

FIVESOME

A group consisting of five players.

FLAGSTICK
The object located on the green to show the position of the hole.

FLOP SHOT
A high shot used in the short game.

FLYER LIE
A lie in the rough that will cause a ball to fly further when hit.

FORE
A warning to other players that a ball has been hit in their direction.

FORECADDIE
A person who alerts other players as to the position of their ball.

FOURSOME
A group consisting of four players.

FRINGE
A closely mowed portion of grass located around the putting surface.

GALLERY
Spectators involved in watching a golf match.

GIMMIE
A conceded putt given by a fellow golfer.

GOLF COURSE SUPERINTENDENT
The person responsible for taking care of the greens, teeing area, fairways and the overall appearance of the golf course.

GRAIN
A term used to describe grass located on the putting surface. Grain can cause a putt to break a certain way or to be slow or fast.

GREEN
The putting surface at the conclusion of each hole.

GROUND UNDER REPAIR
A portion of a golf course marked off usually by paint or a sign denoting that free relief may be taken without penalty due to maintenance of the area.

HANDICAP / INDEX
The number of strokes given to a player in order to make the playing field equal.

HARDPAN
Ground that is very dry and hard making it more difficult to hit from.

HAZARD
A hazard can be any water hazard or bunker located on the golf course.

HEEL
The portion of the club face closest to the hosel.

HOLE IN ONE
Every golfer's dream.

HONOR
The side or player having priority on the tee because of winning the previous hole or match.

HOOK
A ball traveling severely from right to left for a right handed golfer, or left to right for a left-handed golfer.

HOSEL
Hollow part of club-head socket into which the shaft is fitted at the neck of the club.

LATERAL WATER HAZARD
A body of water defined by red stakes or lines.

LAY UP
A strategic shot used to reduce risk.

LOFT
The angle on which the club face is set from vertical. The loft will influence the extent to which the ball can be lifted in flight.

LONG IRON
Irons used to hit long distances ranging from 180 to 250 yards.

LOOSE IMPEDIMENTS
Objects that are not growing, fixed or embedded, and which may be removed prior to making a stroke.

LOST BALL
A ball that cannot be found in the time allotted by the rules of golf.

MARKER
A person who keeps track of a competitors score.

MATCH PLAY
A golf match determined by individual holes, not total score.

MID IRON
Irons used to hit distances ranging from 140 to 175 yards.

MULLIGAN
An extra ball played after making a poor shot. Mulligans are against the rules of golf and contribute to slow play.

OUT-OF-BOUNDS
A ball that travels outside the playing field which requires another shot be played.

OVER PAR
A total score that exceeds the standard score on any particular hole or round.

OVERCLUB
A shot that travels beyond the intended target.

PAR
Standard score for a hole.

PENALTY STROKE
A stroke, or strokes added to the total score of an individual or side, under the rules of golf.

PGA TOUR
A professional golf tour designed for the professional golfer.

PITCH AND RUN
A low shot used in the short game from around the green.

PLAY THROUGH
A term used to allow the group following to pass in order to speed up play.

PLUGGED
A ball embedded in its own mark.

PRO SHOP
The place where players check in prior to their round.

PROVISIONAL BALL
A ball to be played in the event your ball may be lost or out of bounds.

PULL
A term used signaling a right-handed golfer has caused the ball to go left of its intended target or right of the target for a left handed golfer.

RED TEES
The tee box most commonly used by women golfers.

ROUGH
Heavy or long grass fringing the fairway or green.

SANDBAGGER
A player who plays continuously better than his or her handicap or index.

SCRAMBLE
A format used to help speed up play where everyone hits from the best shot between the players until the ball is holed out.

SECOND CUT
Usually found on higher end courses where an extra level of grass is cut bordering fairways and greens

SENIOR PGA TOUR

A professional golf tour designed for players age 50 and older.

SHANK

A shot hit from the neck or hosel of the club resulting in a poor shot.

SHORT GRASS

Golf jargon used to denote the fairway.

SHORT IRON

Irons used to hit short distances ranging from 90 to 135 yards.

SIGNATURE HOLE

The hole on any particular golf course that highlights the beauty and excitement the course has to offer.

SKINS

A game in which a reward is offered for having the lowest score on a hole played.

SLICE

A ball severely traveling from left to right for a right-handed golfer and right to left for a left-handed golfer.

SNAP HOOK

A ball traveling out of control from right to left for a right-handed golfer or from left to right for a left-handed golfer.

SNOWMAN

A score of 8 on any particular hole.

SOFT SPIKES
A shoe spike commonly required by most golf courses used to protect the putting surface.

STARTER
A person who directs and determines the order of play off the first tee.

TEE BOX
The ground from which a tee shot is hit.

TENDING THE FLAGSTICK
Holding the flagstick in order to help your fellow players see the hole from a distance.

THREESOME
Informal term for a group of three players.

THROUGH LINE
The portion of putting surface located just past the hole of each player's intended line of putt.

THE TURN
Going from the 9th green to the 10th tee.

TOE
The portion of the club face furthest from the hosel.

TRIPLE BOGEY
Score for a hole played in three strokes over par.

TWOSOME
Informal term for two players.

UNDER PAR
A total score that is under the standard score for any particular hole or round.

UNDERCLUB
A shot played short of the intended target.

UNDULATION
Mounds and valleys on a putting surface or fairway.

UP AND DOWN
A term used to describe getting your ball in the hole in two shots from around the green.

WAGGLE
Preliminary action of the body flexing causing the club to move forward and backward.

WATER HAZARD
A body of water defined by yellow stakes or lines.

WHITE TEES
The tee box most commonly used by the average golfer.

"Courtesy and integrity are keystones of the game of golf, and learning the rules of etiquette is as essential to one's enjoyment of the game as is learning the fundamentals of the swing. Jim Simpson has done an exceptionally thorough job of explaining **The Un-Spoken Rules of Golf Etiquette** in a positive, straightforward style that will be welcomed by every golfer, particularly those who are new to the game."

● ● ● ● ●   **Jack Nicklaus**

"I have read, with interest, your manuscript, **"The Un-Spoken Rules of Golf Etiquette,"** and can assure you that I am in agreement with the views you are expressing in your book. Proper conduct and courtesies and the honoring of the traditions and rules of the game are vital to its continuing success and popularity."

● ● ● ● ●   **Arnold Palmer**

"By being a part of the grand game of golf the responsibility of knowing the rules and adhering to proper golf etiquette befalls the beginner as well as the seasoned player. Respect the game by respecting its traditions, and by all means have fun doing it!"   ● ● ● ● ●   **Hale Irwin**

"Mr. Simpson's book should be read by many golfers. Those taking up the game as well as people who have played for years. Its underlying hallmark is consideration for others, which forms the basis for nearly all procedures in golf. Respect other players and the course, and everything should follow."

● ● ● ● ●   **Ben Crenshaw**

"Before my father let me out on the course alone he taught me all the rules of golf, including Etiquette. This book will be part of my son's golf education for sure. Finally a book that will help all golfers enjoy the game more!"   **Davis M. Love, III**

● ● ● ● ●

"**The Un-Spoken Rules of Golf Etiquette** should be required reading for all PGA Tour players. Even Tour players forget the rules and traditions that make golf the great game that it is."   **Hal Sutton**

● ● ● ● ●

"Mr. Simpson has provided a perfect companion to the expert instruction available from PGA Professionals — an awareness of and a courtesy toward our playing partners. Thank you for your attention to those situations that cause us to pause and think before we stroll down the fairway."   **Jim L. Awtrey,**
Chief Executive Officer - PGA of America

● ● ● ● ●

"Learning the basics of proper golf etiquette, critical to providing a lifetime of enjoyment on the golf course, is too often overlooked as new players are exposed to our game. **The Un-Spoken Rules of Golf Etiquette** provides a wealth of valuable information and should be required reading for even the most seasoned of golf enthusiasts"

Timothy W. Finchem
Commissioner - PGA Tour

"In an ever changing world of competitive sport there seems to be a modern trend where winning is everything. Fortunately, the one thing that separates golf from all other sports is etiquette. From the first time a golfer picks up a golf club they are made aware of golf course etiquette. As a junior golfer I was very quick to learn that manners on the golf course were an integral part of playing the game. Learning to respect your partners or competitors time to play was, and still is, very important. Not to move or talk while they are playing teaches a junior a very valuable lesson early on. In fact, if the rules and etiquette on the golf course were applied in everyday life, we would all be better off for it."

Nick Price

• • • • •

"**The Un-Spoken Rules of Golf Etiquette** should be read by every golfer at every level. This book should reside in golf bags all over the world to help players enjoy this great game even more." **Peter Jacobsen**

• • • • •

"I've always been a firm advocate of proper golf etiquette and maintaining the tradition of the game. **The Un-Spoken Rules of Golf Etiquette** provide some valuable insight and information, which should be a basic staple for every beginner or junior golfer to read."

Tom Weiskopf

• • • • •

"If everyone followed "**The Un-Spoken Rules of Golf Etiquette**," we'd all play a faster, more enjoyable and better game of golf. And wouldn't we all like to do that?"

Ty M. Votaw
LPGA - Commissioner

• • • • •

"This book has captured the essence of teaching someone the etiquette of the game. It should be required reading before you ever take your first step onto a golf course!"

Thomas A. Morgan, Executive Director
Southern California Golf Association

• • • • •

"Every golfer should read this book — more than once!" **Ely Callaway**

• • • • •

"This is a <u>must read</u>, not only for beginning golfers, but for all golfers!"

Tom Gustafson
Executive Director/CEO
Southern California Section

• • • • •

"As millions continue to enjoy the most civilized sport on our planet, the game of golf is fortunate to receive your commitment to making the game even more enjoyable. The "**Un-Spoken Rules of Golf Etiquette**" offers every generation of golfer the opportunity to truly understand this beloved game and the way the game should be played."

James B. Singerling, CCM, CEC
Chief Executive Officer
Club Managers Association of America

181

"Remember:
All of the Un-Spoken Rules
apply all of the time
regardless of which hole
or what course you are playing"

JAMES SIMPSON

Share This Book with a Friend!

Order Today!
877-360-5800
or

Order directly
from our website:
www.mygolfetiquette.com